C000244369

Walks with Crete's Spring Flowers

Jeff Collman

**A path out of Loutro under a carob tree, the island of
Gavados on the horizon**

Walks with Crete's Spring Flowers

Jeff Collman

Beechwood Press

First published in Great Britain by Beechwood Press, 2003

The right of Jeff Collman to be identified as the author of this work
has been asserted by him in accordance with the Copyright,
Design and Patents Act 1988

All rights reserved. No part of this publication may be reproduced in any
form or by any means, without the prior permission of the copyright holder.

© Jeff Collman 2003

British Library Cataloguing-in-Publication Data
A catalogue record for this book is available from the British Library

ISBN 0-9545988-0-6

Beechwood Press
21 Beechwood Avenue
Newton Abbot
Devon
England
TQ12 4LJ

Typeset by Kestrel Data, Exeter

Printed and bound in Great Britain
by Short Run Press Ltd, Exeter

Contents

Acknowledgements

I wish to thank the many people who have either directly or indirectly enabled this book to be produced. Frances Whistler was the 'final catalyst', who encouraged me to put pen to paper, bribing me with her kind offer to act as editor.

Whilst in Crete, based at Loutro, I have stayed at the Porto Loutro Hotel with Stavros and Alison Androulakakis; and when based at Paleohora I have stayed at the Aris Hotel with Aris Liatakis and his family: in both establishments I have received more care and trust than could be deemed reasonable from hotels. At the Neos Omalos Hotel, where my visits have been brief, my groups have been looked after well by the Drakoulakis family; and Anna Papadakis, the manageress of the Xiloskala restaurant, has been very supportive. There are many locals who have been helpful, often whose names I do not know, but this does not detract from my sense of gratitude towards them; and certainly it has been such behaviour that engenders a feeling of safety and well-being in this area of Crete.

Besides revisiting south west Crete so many times, I have had the added privilege of leading small groups of people on these walks; the company has never been boring, and often inspirational.

Grateful thanks to Barbara Whitaker for financial support.

Particular thanks to Mike Pill, my neighbour, who was the 'guinea-pig' for the Loutro walks, and to Karl-Heinz Classen who provided much information for the Paleohora walks; and to my wife and family for their company in some years, and allowing me the licence to go in the other years.

Preface

That there were several reasons for writing this book does not detract from the validity of any one of them.

For walkers this may form the basic plan for one or more holidays in south-western Crete.

Those interested in flowers may find some of the photographs useful for identification: there will be, however, obviously no attempt made at a complete floral list.

I hope some readers will be sufficiently inspired to visit the area – in Spring (late March to early May) – and for those who have already experienced some or all of the walks, I trust the book will rekindle memories.

Another aspect of this book is as a historical record: there is development taking place in this area. Within the last ten years a vehicular track has reached Livaniana, and also the Gialiskari beaches. The nature of both locations has changed slightly, and probably more change will follow.

In more technical vein: botanical nomenclature has generally followed N.J. Turland, L. Chilton, and J.R. Press: Flora of the Cretan Area annotated checklist & atlas, The Natural History Museum, HMSO, 1993. There are departures however, in that I have used, for example, 'chionodoxa', where the name is very familiar in the horticultural milieu and would be widely evocative (as opposed to 'Scilla' which puts us near a doubtful bluebell). Also I have retained the use of the 'ae' in **Anchusa caespitosa** rather than adopting the more fashionable 'cespitosa': this is to retain information within the nomenclature, and to avoid misinformation. The specific name of a plant is often descriptive, as is the case here, the 'caespitose' condition meaning 'growing in tufts or patches', or 'to do with turf'. A significant feature of **Anchusa caespitosa** is its form, which is a very low growing patch, eminently suitable for avoiding being eaten by herbivores that browse turfs. The spelling 'cespitosa' – at least in the English speaking world – is likely to recall drains, which is a less than helpful association.

The photographs of flowers in this book are usually reduced in size compared with real life: where this is not the case this is mentioned in the picture's caption.

Photographs were nearly all taken by me, or on my camera by another walker of our group; on several occasions the 'other walker' was my wife, Susan. The photographs were taken over a period of ten years, and thus the weather and lighting conditions at the same location have varied: this is evident in some apparently consecutive views; though in one case morning and evening photographs at the same location have been deliberately included: the reason, I hope, will be obvious.

I am very grateful to Leon Lovett for allowing me to use his photographs of walkers on pages ii, and 43.

I trust the reader will appreciate and enjoy this very personal account of small group walks that I have led in south-west Crete for ten years.

Introduction

This book may encourage some people to go walking in Crete in the Spring (late March to early May); that would be my delight: my concern is that some may be ill-prepared and take unnecessary risks.

Dos and Don'ts

Remember that one of the reasons for choosing Crete for walking in Spring is the climate; generally warm and sunny – so attractive to north-western Europeans. But this *can* be a source of danger, in that an otherwise minor accident of, for example, twisting one's ankle, can become life threatening if dehydration or salt depletion sets in. With the best will in the world, rescue services, such as they are, take time to reach casualties; I believe that it is prudent always to be equipped as though one could spend a night 'in the field' – or rather on a path! This is not so cumbersome as one might imagine, since night temperatures are generally mild (except above Omalos).

Thus my advice is:
- Always carry water, in several stout containers e.g. plastic fizzy-drink bottles (they are built to withstand pressure, and do not break easily in a fall – unlike ordinary water bottles – and there is safety in numbers). About 2 litres of water for a day is not unreasonable.
- Always carry food; tomatoes, bananas and citrus fruit will help with salt balance.
  And by saying 'always carry', I mean that one should be carrying food and water on the *return* journey, as well as the outward one. Accidents are MORE likely when one is tired.
- Always carry a lightweight waterproof; showers can be heavy and blowy; and if one did have to overnight, this, as an outer layer, would provide good insulation against chilly breezes.
- Thick-soled footwear with a good grip is advisable; some paths have sharp uneven surfaces; some places may be polished smooth.
- Sunscreens should be worn; burning is often not noticed whilst walking, especially in Crete where there is so often a cooling breeze.

- A torch and a whistle should be carried; the torch to enable one to be *found* in the dark, not to find one's way.
- Last, but certainly not of least importance, one should not walk alone.

Telling someone the day's proposed route and anticipated time of return is also wise, as is walking in groups; beyond three people in a group there is the possibility of the injured party not being left alone as others seek help. Mobile phones of course have improved communication considerably in the last few years; but one needs to remember that in such hilly/mountainous terrain signal strengths vary greatly.

If you are reading this book cover to cover, or are planning to do all of the walks sequentially, then you will notice that I have separated the Paleohora walks by the Samaria Gorge and Gingilos Mountain walks. This is deliberate positioning to emphasise that it is *not* a good idea to walk down the Samaria Gorge on the last day of your holiday. If the sirocco blows (a south east wind, quite frequent in Spring, and usually stormy) the ferry boats from Agia Roumeli may not sail; and since there are no roads into or out of Agia Roumeli, you will be stranded there, at least for one night.

Having dealt briefly with self preservation, we should also consider the preservation of what we, as tourists, visit. If paths are to be maintained they need to be used, or they may become overgrown; and they need to be seen to be used or the built-up sections will be allowed to collapse, since their use by local inhabitants is minimal and decreasing. So, what a pleasant 'duty' we bestow upon ourselves by visiting this area; but of course paths are only a minor feature of the landscape. The way the landscape appears now, is, to a large extent, the product of past and present types of agriculture. The many areas that have abandoned terraces are witness to an earlier regime of intensive arable cultivation. More recently these terraces have been used as extensions of rough grazing for sheep and goats. However, during the last 50 years, tourism has been very profitable, and certainly perceived as more glamorous than farming. Since it seems neither feral sheep nor goats thrive in Crete, the effect of the movement of labour from agriculture to tourism has been a reduction of grazing pressure. Many of Crete's rare and interesting plants of the herbaceous layer depend upon the shrubs and trees being kept in check by grazing. Thus if we ask for goat (which is actually very good) in a taverna, it may be provided, and therefore the likelihood of goat-herding continuing increases, which indirectly maintains the herbaceous plants' habitat. Fire is another great factor in determining vegetation-cover types, and is deliberately used (in a controlled manner – swaling) to encourage new growth for grazing near ground level whilst preventing the formation of a tall shrub and tree canopy. With an increase in tourism, accidental fires are likely to increase in frequency. This is probably detrimental to many herbaceous plants in the long term since, without grazing pressure, **Pinus brutia** is quick to regenerate after a fire, and the ground flora under its canopy is not rich.

The urbanisation of the landscape due to tourism is driven by the numbers of summer visitors. A better return on capital invested (accommodation is empty for much of the year) could be obtained if the tourist season were extended by visitors interested in the rural wild areas and their unique flora. These 'natural' assets are becoming increasingly rare, and are, in the long term, financially worth maintaining. In spring-time, being less busy, the locals have more time to talk, and listen to our reasons for visiting this very special area.

As visitors we probably do least damage to the environment by, whenever possible, patronising local businesses and services.

Beyond talking to the local people about their unique flora – quite remarkable in world terms – I have often found it difficult (not being a speaker of Greek) to show interest in flowers without unintended and undesirable consequences. I stopped to admire a rural garden with some massive roses and lilies; the woman owner, with an even larger generosity of spirit, rushed and cut them for our group of walkers. Ecologically worse, showing interest in an orchid, can result in being presented with a bunch of them – enough to stock a nature reserve in England!

This book is not a step by step guide, the like of which tends to be out of date before it's in print; and I fear encourages a nose-in-book approach to the countryside, rather than an exploring spirit. Having said that, I hope the book will be useful in giving people both the inspiration and the confidence to set forth; along with snippets of information where nerves might otherwise have failed!

The vast majority of the walks are on either way-marked paths or vehicular tracks or roads. It is almost never a good idea to depart from these tracks. If you lose the way-marks (blobs of coloured paint), try to retrace your steps to the last paint blob, then stand still and look; paint way-marks are often within sight lines of each other. Cairns are also often used to mark paths; in some areas they have become an art form in themselves. Sheep and goats can be good path makers, but after what may feel like miles, their paths have a habit of vanishing, rather in the middle of nowhere; fortunately they do not also use paint or cairns.

Why 'Walk with Crete's Spring Flowers'? Well, there are many good reasons. The climate is generally sunny and warm, often with a cooling breeze. The flowers in springtime are numerous and more diverse than in Britain. The mountainous nature of the island provides frequently-changing vistas and great habitat diversity, not to mention the snowy peaks' glistening appeal. The beaches are not crowded and provide civilized cooling breaks. The areas I visit have a low population density, so there's a good sense of 'getting away from (most of) it all'.

With the exception of the last sentence, all these reasons could equally be applied to many Mediterranean islands e.g. Majorca, Corsica, Sardinia, Corfu and Cyprus: but Crete *is* significantly different.

The climate of Crete has its extremes tempered slightly by its position away from the three main continents. The southern coast is sheltered from northerly influences by the east-west ridge of mountains, and can be noticeably warmer in Spring than the north coast; and in the Summer, when temperatures soar, there is usually a cooling breeze. Crete is further south than other major Mediterranean islands, indeed its off-island of Gavdos is the southernmost part of Europe.

The flowers of Crete are very special, primarily because of the high level of endemism. The island has more endemic plants than any other European island. An endemic plant is one that grows naturally only in the defined area and nowhere else in the world. The Cretan area (Crete, Karpathos and nearby islands) has approximately 1700 species of 'higher' plants (plants that evolved later than Pteridophytes, which include ferns), and of these approximately 10% are endemics. This fact alone probably guarantees a steady stream of botanists visiting Crete: but this phenomenon is of very long standing. We know that there was interest in Crete's flora at least from the 4th Century BC, from the writings of Theophrastus; and by the 18th Century there was sufficient collection of botanical specimens from Crete for many to be given the specific name 'cretica'. This is perhaps not at all surprising for a Cretan endemic such as **Ebenus cretica**; but for **Bryonia cretica** (a plant *not* confined to the Cretan area) to be so named by Linnaeus (who never visited Crete, or indeed the Mediterranean), one suspects that during the

18th Century the 'botanical fame' of Crete had become a little exaggerated.

The Cretan mountains were separated from the adjoining continents for the last time approximately 5 million years ago (during the Pliocene when the Mediterranean area became a sea); and approximately 1 million years ago (during the Lower Pleistocene) the island had virtually its present-day shape. Thus, isolated flora and fauna on Crete had about 5 million years to evolve relatively independently from the continents. Much of the vegetation would have been subjected to heavy grazing pressure, since there were many herbivores (including the now extinct Cretan elephants, hippopotami, giant rodents and several species of deer), but no carnivores larger than the badger. Thus plants that developed an unpleasant taste or are poisonous, such as **Nerium oleander**, or developed spines such as the Cretan endemic **Verbascum spinosum,** were at a selective advantage. These contrast with other plants (chasmophytes) which evolved in the many gorges (or chasms) where major herbivores could not reach them, and lack these defence

**Petromarula pinnata and Verbascum arcturus
both Cretan endemic chasmophytes**

mechanisms. Examples of these are the Cretan endemics **Ebenus cretica**, **Petromarula pinnata** and **Verbascum arcturus** all of which are becoming more widespread now that grazing pressure is decreasing.

There is an easily identifiable mix of the continental origins of the flora: **Ebenus cretica** and **Zelkova abelicea** are both Cretan endemic species belonging to genera with centres of distributions in Asia; **Arum cyrenaicum**, found in Crete, is otherwise found in North Africa; and of the genus Cyclamen which is well represented in the Aegean, there is the Cretan endemic **Cyclamen creticum**. Even the Cretan cypress **Cupressus sempervirens** naturally grows no further west than Crete; it is otherwise scattered over mountain ranges to Iran (and this is the species, in its columnar form, which is known as the 'Italian cypress'!).

The dramatic topography of Crete allows us in Spring to walk, within one day (if determined and fit), from snowfields with drifts of crocus and chionodoxa; through carpets of cyclamen, to poppies and oleander flowering near the coast. In terms of British floristic norms, this is like walking from January to July (Physically one can walk up Gingilos Mountain and down the Samaria Gorge in one, very long, day: aesthetically it is *not* recommended).

The mountains of Crete are high: Ida is 2456m, Pakhnes 2453m, and as well as Pakhnes, the Levka Ori (White Mountains) boast some 20 peaks over 2000m. By world standards these may not seem very great; but what makes the perceived height, particularly of the White Mountains, so impressive, is their proximity to the sea without an intervening 'foothill zone'.

Viewing this mountainous island, as one flies in for a walking holiday, can be daunting; but the island's long history of civilization has resulted in many paths and donkey tracks (kalderimi) being constructed. These long-used paths usually have relatively gentle gradients, and tame many a fearsome mountainside with their zigzags.

Besides providing visual grandeur, the east-west mountain ridge of Crete also has a significant effect on the climate of the island. In Summer it is often the focus for storms, and the annual rainfall on the mountains is higher than on the surrounding lowlands, especially those to the north and east.

The White Mountains are composed predominantly of limestone, and thus drainage is largely by underground streams and rivers. The higher areas are relatively devoid of vegetation and soil cover, though specialised mountain species have evolved that do inhabit these areas (but *not* of the European Arctic-Alpine flora).

The beaches of south-west Crete are very appealing to many spring-time walkers, as much a means of cooling off as a goal in themselves. Refreshing the sea certainly is at this time of year, recently fed by snow melt water from the mountains; but the great joy is that on emerging from the sea, one is virtually assured of warming up quickly.

Low population density. One of the aims of many walkers is to escape the madding crowd. With the one notable exception of the Samaria Gorge walk, all other walks should achieve this goal. Even if the publication of this book increases the use of the described paths by a factor of two, there will still be plenty of space and peace.

1. Half-day walk: Loutro to Likkos

Before writing about this walk, I must recount my first experience of walking from Loutro. It was, I thought, quite well planned, in that I had found out the times of the boats (I was just a day visitor); and had read guide books. I knew that I wanted to walk to 'Marble Beach' (Marmara) and back; and from the timings given in a widely available 'Walks' book, this was a very reasonable objective. Of course I had been to Crete before, walking and looking at flowers; so I was reasonably well equipped regarding footwear, food and drink. So what, besides physical accidents could go wrong? I had not anticipated the 'Loutro Factor'.

Approaching Loutro

My first view of Loutro, the year before, as for most visitors, had been from the ferryboat to Agia Roumeli. As the boat approaches from Hora Sfakion, it makes straight for a small cluster of white dots, which develop into a small cluster of whitewashed buildings in a horseshoe bay. Instead of the boat veering to another bearing point, it heads straight for the pebble beach: it's possibly the date palm that it steers for! The ferryboat is big: Loutro is small, and immediately appealing. I resolved to get off the boat next time. So when the 'next time' arrived, 12 months later, disembarkation at Loutro was quite a thrill. To be part of the bustle of provisions and visitors leaving the boat was a heady experience. The boat pulls out, turns, and becomes of respectable proportions as it heads for Agia Roumeli; and suddenly one realises that there are very few people around, and the delight of Loutro is almost one's own.

The major paths out of Loutro go inland from near the 'kiosk', a small pebble's throw from where I stood. At a diminutive 'general store' the left hand fork is the westward path. In springtime it may be bordered with mounds of yellow and white **Chrysanthemum coronarium**, some very floriferous mauve **Malva sylvestris**, and brilliant red poppies (**Papaver rhoeas**). Having stopped, the eye may rise to the bright green leaves of a pomegranate bush (**Punica granatum**) with a few vivid orange flowers close to **Nerium oleander** bushes possibly sporting some early pink flowers, above this a date palm (**Phoenix dactylifera**) makes part of the skyline with the village church. It is warm, sunny, quiet (there are no cars – there are no roads!), and definitely not England. The path leads past a small shrine to a makeshift gate: yes, goats have been a significant factor in determining the vegetation cover of this area, and, to protect courtyard gardens and probably tourists from continual harassment, are excluded from Loutro. Just beyond the gate are some ancient olive trees. They have massive gnarled trunks, some partially hollow. I learnt later that one has been dated by ring counting, and would have been growing here in the Hellenistic period, from the 3rd century BC. The sense of different time scales is extraordinary: within a few minutes Loutro beach, on a ferry schedule, transforms from a bustling highway to tranquillity; these olive trees, probably nurtured by a pre-Roman culture, were mature when the Venetians built their arsenal (now used as a laundry) here in Loutro, their culture to be replaced by a succession of others, including ours. It was all too easy to stand and stare in surroundings that are so captivating; and, photograph, to try to

Loutro village church, with oleander, pomegranate, date and olive

preserve the moment – take selectively of course, minus cables and wire netting! Beyond this point the path becomes zigzagged and stepped to gain height; then reaches the 'cliff top' near the site of the Venetian castle.

The view to the east is immediately demanding. On a clear day in Spring like this, the snow-capped peak of Mount Ida is the distant focus: Hora Sfakion is in the middle distance, and on the ridge of mountains to the north one can pick out the site railings of St. Catherine's Church.

By the castle there are flowers of **Dracunculus vulgaris** 'Dragon lily' (don't stand down wind of a mature flower – it smells like rotting goat). To the east are open areas that could be called grassland, but for the fact that on closer inspection they are found to have a high proportion of showier flowering plants, usually dancing in a pleasant breeze.

It was by the Venetian castle that on this first walk from Loutro I looked at my watch. I found I had taken more than half the time allocated to reach Marble Beach (a few horizontal miles distant), to get myself a matter of a few hundred yards away from Loutro. I resolved to stay at Loutro and not look at my watch.

View eastwards, from near Loutro's Venetian castle

Loutro's Venetian castle

Dracunculus vulgaris, with Phoenix church

From the castle it's an easy walk to Phoenix, a west-facing bay on the other side of the headland from Loutro. In ancient times this headland was the site of a significant port, providing shelter in harbours facing west or east, and serving the large population inland at the agriculturally rich Anopoli which is only a mile or so beyond the ridge of the northern skyline.

The path to Phoenix; Livaniana is near the skyline

The path drops down to Phoenix, a very minor modern development; or one can bypass it. Beyond Phoenix, paint way-marks indicate a division of the ways by a Carob tree (**Ceratonia siliqua**), and if one keeps towards the coast the next habitation is at Likkos Bay. Past a few tavernas, the path crosses the back of a beach and then abruptly reaches the foot of a cliff. There are steps upwards; but for a first walk from Loutro, this can be a suitable stop or picnic point.

The return to Loutro, retracing one's steps, can take a considerable time if all four tavernas are patronised.

2. Loutro to Anopoli and Sweetwater Beach

Loutro, from where the outward and homeward paths divide

The scale of scenery around Loutro is staggering.
Arrival at Loutro, whether from Chania or Herakleion airport is

usually via the Imbros Gorge road to Hora Sfakion. This passes through dramatic mountain scenery, and in the gorge itself becomes a series of hairpin bends. I always hope my taxi man will heed my pleas for slow driving. If flight times are 'unfortunate', arrival at Hora Sfakion may be after the last ferry to Loutro: no matter: it's likely a small boat will be sent out. It was on such an evening when we were making headway in quite a distinct swell, that I remember long-time 'Loutrophile' Julie Friedeberger enthusiastically pointing out to first-time walkers that the faintly discernable pencil line on the towering cliff face would be their path to Sweetwater Beach, while of course the path to Anopoli would take them up over the horizon. For those already showing signs of a greenish hue, this must have felt like the last straw.

But after a gentle first day's walk to Likkos Bay (see Walk 1.), and two breakfasts under one's belt, the prospect is perhaps still daunting, but has expectations of compensating delights.

Asphodeline lutea

The path begins by the kiosk on the pebble beach as for Walk 1, but for Anopoli one takes the right-hand fork. This path passes between gardens and across 'courtyards' before reaching the north eastern gate. Just past a ruin on the right-hand side, the path forks again – the right-hand one being our route home. The left one strikes upwards and becomes stepped, and faced with stones in a way one would expect of a major route that has been used for thousands of years. The gradient is not steep, the zigzags are long, and in Spring many flowers can be seen on what had appeared from a distance to be very barren ground.

There is usually the sound of goat bells and an ever-changing view of Loutro.

Loutro, with its castle on the horizon

The small bright yellow-green flowers of **Euphorbia acanthothamnos** appear to be emerging through a hexagonal mesh of spines (looking very much like wire netting). This method of spiny branch growth, as a means of deterring grazing, is also found in **Sarcopoterium spinosum** (a member of the Rosaceae); an obvious case

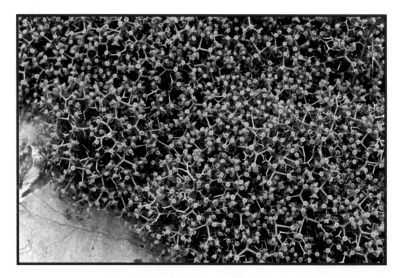

Euphorbia acanthothamnos

of convergent evolution. **Sarcopoterium spinosum** is easily distinguished by its reddish and duller-yellow flower heads.

At about the point where the path is joined by the route from Phoenix, the view shows the full extent of the Loutro peninsula and the relative positions of the Loutro and Phoenix bays.

If you make an early start after breakfast, a good height can be reached before the sun rises above the horizon. The extra heat is a mixed blessing: if there is little wind, it's not long before thermals start to form – not powerful, but much appreciated by hot and tired walkers, especially at the edges of exposed bends. Often it's not only walkers that make use of these thermals. At about the time of losing the view of Loutro, it is worth scanning the skyline above, where golden eagles often patrol, and ravens are usually heard. Griffon vultures also soar here, but this is a less dependable occurrence. The path crosses over a vehicular track (to a 'sheep hotel' – a long low concrete block structure), and eventually has a sharp turning off to the left. Ignoring this, follow the rather less well-defined path over more open country to a gap between two areas enclosed by stone walls, topped with wire netting.

**Dracunculus vulgaris, white form, beside the path
from Loutro to Anopoli**

Loutro and its peninsula; a church at its eastern tip, Phoenix bay to the west.

It is here that the magic of Anopoli begins. From what had been the occasional joy of flowers in rather bare countryside, suddenly the flowers become abundant, and with the grazing pressure from sheep and goats reduced, the fenced areas provide a feast for the eyes.

As one approaches the first houses, a frequent factor of Cretan walking will be encountered – the guard dog. It is usually tethered, but very vocal; one suspects it is here as signal as well as guard, since just around the corner there is usually a lady selling lace to passing walkers.

At this point one feels in another world of lushness and plenty. Small fields are planted with crops; artichokes give a rather exotic touch to the landscape, and snow-capped mountains, perhaps unnoticed at first, provide a backdrop for photographs.

The path becomes a road that leads to a T-junction with the main road from Hora Sfakion to Anopoli and Aradena. Turning left we eventually come to the main square of Anopoli, but not before passing many botanical delights.

**Chrysanthemum coronarium, both yellow
and white forms, at Anopoli**

Salvia fruticosa and Phlomis fruticosa at Anopoli

13

Echium italicum

Barlia robertiana

Lupinus pilosus, olive trees and sheep at Anopoli

Opuntia ficus-barbarica, Olea europaea and Cupressus sempervirens at Anopoli

15

**Anemone coronaria as an
agricultural weed at Anopoli**

Gladiolus italicus with yellow composites, as weeds at Anopoli

Anopoli is a good place for refreshment and rest in tavernas, either in its square, or 100 metres further along the Aradena road. The square is unexpectedly large for the size of the village. Anopoli was formerly a much larger town: even now its population is scattered over a wide area, not just centred on the main road.

The imposing bust in the square is of Dhaskaloyiannis, who was born in Anopoli, and who in 1770 led an unsuccessful Cretan rebellion against the occupying Turks, for which he was executed.

The next leg of this walk is to go back along the road towards Hora Sfakion, to join the path to Sweetwater Beach and Loutro. From where we joined the main road this morning, to the Sweetwater path, the relatively new, multi-hair-pinned asphalt road has obliterated parts of the old donkey track, and is *not* a pleasant walk. There is a bus that serves Anopoli – but timing is then a restriction: much the best idea is to arrange transport – lift – taxi – almost anything with wheels – before setting off from Loutro (both the tavernas on or near the square are on the telephone).

The Sweetwater path leaves the road at one of the westernmost hairpin bends; there will probably be a few cars parked, and it is signposted. Indeed an earlier E4 coastal path sign here was featured on a quality postcard, partly for the impressive background scenery, but mostly for the lacework effect caused by locals shooting at the sign for target practice. **Verbascum spinosum**, a Cretan endemic, usually flowers here on south facing slopes earlier in the season than elsewhere.

For those who ever suffer from vertigo, this is a good place to plan. Make sure you are not suffering from dehydration or salt loss by drinking and eating (tomatoes and / or bananas being particularly suitable): and do not lead the way (followers have their sightlines partially obstructed, which usually helps). I am a vertigo sufferer myself, and it can have advantages: I was once being ultra-cautious, not looking at the distant views and only focussing on the nearside cliff as I progressed virtually hand over hand on this section of path, when I was faced with the exquisite sight of **Solenopsis minuta** flowers.

In subsequent years I have controlled my vertigo sufficiently to photograph them, and also the overhanging **Ebenus cretica**, another Cretan endemic, which usually flowers here early in the season.

The views along this section of the coast are very dramatic, and can be somewhat surreal in that there is little with which to maintain one's sense of scale. Ravens are often seen here, and, less frequently, Griffon vultures: not the most reassuring of company!

Verbascum spinosum (Cretan endemic)

**Solenopsis minuta
(approx. life-size)**

Ebenus cretica (Cretan endemic) overhanging the path

Sweetwater Beach is a long stretch of pebbles and gravel, dwarfed by the towering cliffs behind. In places the sedimentary banding of the rocks is very noticeable, and is found to support **Capparis spinosa** (capers – it is the young flower buds that are eaten) with its delicate flowers, as well as **Verbascum arcturus** and **Centaurea argentea**.

19

Sweetwater Beach

Capparis spinosa

Centaurea argentea

21

Sweetwater Beach's name relates to the fresh water springs that run into the sea at or just below the pebble surface at the western end. This spring water is now piped to Loutro. On a hot day the sea is very inviting for swimming, but don't expect the sea temperature to be warm; these springs are not many miles from snow melt on the Levka Ori.

The early setting of the sun behind the high cliffs is usually the signal to take the path that rises steeply from the western end of the beach. It's approximately an hour's walk to Loutro. There may be diversions on the way, for example to visit the church to the seaward side of the main path, or simply to contemplate the views in the setting sun.

The path from Sweetwater to Loutro; Hora Sfakion in the distance

Approaching Loutro, goat bells are one's company: the goatherd has the easternmost property in Loutro. The usual experience as one enters the village is long shadows, amber eyes, and a cacophony of bells.

Cove on the path to Loutro (photographed in the morning)

**Nerium oleander on the path to Loutro
(photographed in the morning)**

3. Loutro to Livaniana, Aradena Gorge and Marble Beach

This walk should not be one's first walk from Loutro; the way-marking is at times faint, there is some scrambling, and possible danger of vertigo: however it would be a huge loss to omit it.

Assuming that one has walked to Phoenix before (Walk 1), progress can be relatively brisk to the point beyond Phoenix where, near a carob tree, the coastal path leaves a right-hand turning. It is this right-hand fork to Livaniana that is our new ground. Soon after going through a gate, and maybe passing a display of **Convolvulus althaeoides**, the path becomes a recognisably paved ancient way that zigzags upwards to Livaniana. The new road track has obliterated the top end of the path;

Convolvulus althaeoides

24

but has brought refreshment and electricity to the village, and a new taverna. The village of Livaniana had almost become abandoned before the road was constructed, but the beautiful site, with almond and olive trees, can also be home to nightingales and golden orioles.

View of Phoenix and Likkos Bay from the path to Livaniana

At the top of the village the church is worth a visit; even if it is not open, there is a good view from its yard. Beyond the church, and ignoring a right-hand path between walls and fences, there is an abrupt right-hand turn, which leads to the church of St. Athanasius – visible in the distance up the gorge, below the high mountains.

Terraces to the left of the path here above Livaniana have been subjected to a regime of partial grazing which has favoured **Chrysanthemum segetum**. This provides a colourful display in Spring.

Terraces above Livaniana, with the church of St. Athanasius in the distance

Echium plantagineum, Papaver rhoeas, and Chrysanthemum segetum on terraces above Livaniana

Red form of Ranunculus asiaticus flowering on the abandoned terraces, above Livaniana, on the side of the Aradena Gorge; the island of Gavdos faintly visible on the horizon

27

Ignoring a path that branches to the left down into the gorge, our way is to the church. The terracing and path are in rather poor condition; though evidence of relatively recent cultivation is still here, in that some of the fruit trees are grafted.

The church of St. Athanasius (who was the author of a widely used creed) is certainly quietly situated, but has been relatively recently renovated.

Beyond the church are delightful terraces with some shade, making them an ideal place for a picnic lunch. Your only companions are likely to be sheep, and the calls of ravens and cuckoos.

View from near the church of St Athanasius

Suitably refreshed, it's worth investigating the terraces above the path that leads towards the gorge. Their vegetative cover appears to be almost a pure stand of **Sarcopoterium spinosum**, but on closer investigation (wearing tough foot/ankle/leg wear) you should find one of the less common plants, **Ophrys heldreichii**, some specimens being quite a dark pink.

Ophrys heldreichii
(about twice life size)

The path drops quite steeply into the Aradena Gorge whose floor supports many bushes of **Vitex agnus-castus**, a shrub which prefers to have its roots near the water table (it flowers in summer), and which, in Spring, has mostly bare branches.

At this point it is worth considering gorge formation.

It is thought that many gorges in limestone country (e.g. Cheddar Gorge in England) were formed by the roof collapsing into the bed of what had been an underground river which originally cut its way through the limestone largely by solution. But in Crete this is not thought to be the main causal factor for the formation of so many predominantly north-south gorges. It is suggested that cracks were formed by large blocks of rock pushing against each other and then splitting (much as cheese cracks). So the whole island could have been subjected to lateral (east-west) pressure which has resulted in more or less parallel cracking of the rocks: some cracks (gorges) being very wide; others being narrow.

The Aradena Gorge certainly looks like a crack in the earth's crust; very minor in geological terms, but from a human perspective, it's big enough for us to walk along its floor to appreciate the sense of drama.

The island of Crete has been isolated from other land masses for five million years. During this time the grazing pressure has been considerable, since there were no major carnivores. The result is a characteristic feature of the Cretan flora: numerous plants whose natural habitat is chasm walls where they are not accessible to major grazers. These chasmophytes tend to lack chemical (distasteful / poisonous) or mechanical (spiny) means of protection; whilst having small light seeds that can easily be blown up against chasm walls.

On entering the gorge many examples of chasmophytes will be seen, such as **Verbascum arcturus**, **Ebenus cretica**, and **Securigera globosa**; along with **Linum arboreum** hanging from the cliffs.

Herbaceous gems that can be found in the Aradena Gorge include **Cyclamen creticum** (sometimes in slightly pink forms), **Gagea graeca** (Greek lily), **Ophrys lutea, Ophrys sphegodes subsp. cretensis, Ophrys sphegodes subsp. gortynia, Ophrys heldreichii, Ophrys holoserica, Serapias sp.** (species not determined) and **Ranunculus asiaticus** (which in the gorge is represented by stiff white forms as well as the more common, easily wind-blown types whose colour varies from white to pink-tinged, and a rather greyish yellow).

The Aradena Gorge, seen from where the path from
St Athanasius' church joins. A walker is on the gorge bed

31

**Securigera globosa (Cretan endemic), on the walls of the
Aradena Gorge**

Verbascum arcturus (Cretan endemic)

Ophrys sphegodes subsp. gortynia (Cretan endemic)

Linum arboreum

Ranunculus asiaticus

35

Walkers in the shade; Aradena Gorge

One must, at times, remember to stop and look up. It's all too easy to be intent on secure walking and herb spotting: only when one stops does the relative silence break through, and our senses become attuned to the background hum of bees. The wildness and quiet solitude (one ought not to be walking alone) are invaluable attributes of this gorge.

Much of the walking is on smooth pebbles; there are some points where scrambling is necessary, following way-marks.

Near the sea the gorge walls tower overhead; with many blue spikes of the Cretan endemic chasmophyte, **Petromarula pinnata**: but not all the blue spikes have those masses of spidery flowers. Some, with large, rather open bells (resembling horticultural 'Canterbury bells') are another chasmophyte **Campanula laciniata**.

Campanula laciniata

Rather abruptly the gorge opens out to a small beach – Marmara, or Marble Beach, aptly named because there is an outcrop of marble (shown below) which is smoothly polished by wave action at the shoreline. There is now a taverna overlooking the beach.

If it's calm, and you are not alone, take a swim eastwards from the beach, past the first cave, and into the second one (it has a rectangle scratched on its wall). Swim to the back of this cave, which appears to be closed: only when you are at the back will you see the gap through to the next cave, which you swim into. The lighting will act as your guide; but to see the lighting to *best* effect one needs to be here in the morning.

Marmara or Marble beach

It will probably be tea-time when you emerge from the gorge; either early, or late, depending on the delights encountered. Refreshed from a picnic or the taverna, invigorated by a swim and possibly inspired by the cave; you need to start the journey home before dusk. It's about an hour's walk to Loutro. The route is now the E4 path eastwards that leads to Loutro; easy at first, then gently rising, and later being too close to the edge for the comfort of vertigo sufferers like me. The discomfort is short-lived and ends at the steps that lead down to the beach at Likkos Bay. From here on the path is easy, and probably familiar, since this is the return journey of the first half day's walk (Walk 1). Perhaps this time you will visit another of the tavernas en route – the starlight may be enough to guide you home.

4. Loutro to Agia Roumeli and Agios Pavlos

A daytrip that begins and ends with a ferryboat journey; the walking is partly across beaches and partly under **Pinus brutia**.

If the previous walks described in this book have been undertaken sequentially, then two boat journeys and walking in dappled shade may be a relief; certainly it's a change.

The ferryboat takes one effortlessly past Phoenix, Likkos Bay and Marble Beach, with a good view of the Aradena Gorge (and briefly St. Athanasius' Church), with probably a snow-capped peak as skyline.

The Aradena Gorge from the sea: vegetation cover of the hills, phrygana type

A plan view of the coastline from here, would show it to be gently convexly curved: and the vegetation cover of the hills is mostly a low grazed phrygana. This continues until the coastline retreats beyond a small headland where the vegetation changes abruptly to **Pinus brutia** cover, sea birds may be seen and sometimes a sulphurous odour detected. This is the site of a major geological fault.

From here the skyline towers above the coast: to maintain some sense of scale you need to remember the cliffs are clothed with mature **Pinus brutia** trees (which grow to approx. 10m), and also on the beach is a church (Agios Pavlos) and a taverna – both of which you can only see easily with binoculars.

The foreground headland has phrygana vegetation; beyond the fault there is Pinus brutia woodland

Most of the people who leave the boat at Agia Roumeli, make their way to the Samaria Gorge. If we follow them to where the track takes a sharp left turn to go up the river valley, we will have seen most of the 'resort' of New Agia Roumeli, and hopefully noticed the Turkish castle on the hill above, guarding the gorge entrance.

Our route is to cross the river, but not by the bridge, which is ruined. So we make our way downstream – near the sea there are stepping stones or a makeshift plank bridge. A track then leads eastwards and for some

**Walkers appreciating pine-scented shade
on the path to Agios Pavlos**

time the route crosses a long beach. If the weather is 'good', this section can be very hot and glaring.

Way-marks show the path leading up into **Pinus brutia** woodland which is a refreshingly different experience; not only does one have dappled shade, but also the pine smell. Two shrubs which are commonly found here, and are usually in flower in April, are **Lithodora hispidula** (much more common further west) and **Cistus creticus**.

The church of Agios Pavlos is situated literally on the beach, and the 'well', reputedly blessed by St. Paul, is a fresh-water stream that emerges just above sea level, slightly to the east of the church. Inside the church one is struck by several things: quiet, verticality, and some delightful remnants of frescoes.

Agios Pavlos church

Walkers near Agios Pavlos church

To the west of the church there is now a taverna. The ferry timings are such that one cannot afford to get too comfortable either in the taverna, or warming up after a bracing swim (fresh water wells up along most of the beach, visible as gentle vortices in the seawater, and felt as significantly cold patches). The return walk means retracing one's steps as far as the river crossing; beyond this, keep near the sea to reach the jetty, or the tavernas if time permits. The journey home to Loutro on the ferry is an opportunity to put one's feet up.

For those who enjoy walking per se, the E4 path from Agios Pavlos leads to Loutro via Marble Beach, Likkos Bay and Phoenix. The section from Agios Pavlos to Marble Beach has little in the way of novelty, excepting at the fault area (which there may be insufficient time to investigate!). Maintaining a brisk pace could get you to Loutro before the ferry.

A more luxurious variation may be arranged before setting out from Loutro. If the sea is calm, a small boat can collect you from Agios Pavlos beach, and return you to Loutro in the rays of the setting sun.

5. Loutro to St. Catherine's Church, Anopoli, Aradena and Livaniana

A long circular walk with considerable diversity, using a dramatic section of a well-preserved kalderimi (constructed mule track).

The beginning of this walk is the same as the walk to Anopoli (Walk 2); except that having had that experience, one will probably resolve to start earlier in the morning so that the 'major ascent' is achieved in the cool, and as far as possible without the sun in one's eyes. A very early start has also the huge advantage of seeing the dawn; one's eyes easily accommodate to dim conditions.

Dawn at Loutro

Once the car track has been crossed, instead of following straight on, turn left at the next fork to zigzag upwards. Quite suddenly the snow-

Levka Ori seen from across the Anopoli plain

capped panorama of the Levka Ori appears across the Anopoli plain.
This ridge-pass is a very obvious place for a snack and photographic
break before continuing upwards to St Catherine's Church, which is
usually open. The view from the yard is spectacular. It's often worth
lingering here awhile, since golden eagles or griffon vultures may stage
a fly-past, either above or below.

From here the path, which becomes a road, descends into Anopoli.
The vegetation on the left-hand side is worth watching; I have
sometimes found **Orchis pauciflora** here, but **Ophrys lutea** is much
more likely, along with a host of **Gagea graeca**, and possibly a yellow
Gagea sp. The road leads into the village, under a walnut tree, and into
the main square. The taverna here, or the one 100 metres further on up
the road to Aradena on the left, can make an excellent second breakfast
stop.

The Aradena road is easy walking, but there are many distractions.
Almost immediately past the taverna at the road junction, on the
left-hand side, may be a good display of **Iris albicans**; many of the fields
and olive groves have **Anemone coronaria**, both purple and red forms,

46

Ophrys lutea (approximately life-size)

Gagea graeca (Greek lily) approximately life-size

47

Poppies and the Levka Ori above Anopoli

**Ranunculus asiaticus: note the sepals, which are not present in
Anemone. The apparently 'white zone', is in fact high lustre**

the latter being easily confused with the red form of **Ranunculus
asiaticus** which is also in the fields here. Generally later in the season,
but certainly overlapping in period, are the similarly red flowers of
Papaver rhoeas; but these tend to be more delicately textured and thus
move in very slight breezes, whereas both Anemone and the RED form
of **Ranunculus asiaticus** tend to be stiffer and more wind-resistant.
(The normal 'type' white form of **R. asiaticus** is very prone to being
moved by breezes – it is called the 'wind flower'.)

On the right-hand side of the road, by a shrine, **Rosmarinus
officinalis** (rosemary) flourishes for remembrance. **Gynandriris
sisyrinchium** may provide splashes of blue that are as arresting as those
of **Anchusa italica**. **Ophrys lutea** is usually found, as are **Orchis
collina, Orchis coriophora subsp. fragrans** and **Serapias sp.**: **Orchis
pauciflora** is also recorded from this area. **Eryngium campestre** is

Orchis pauciflora

very frequently found here – giving the impression of a misplaced sea
holly.

Whilst plant-hunting in these olive groves, do watch out for bird-life;
hoopoes are seen here.

Just before the road passes through a small hamlet with its own church
and a collection of stately mature **Quercus coccifera** (kermes or holly
oak) trees, there are rather lush green bushes of **Anagyris foetida** on the
left hand side of the road; but identify without too much handling: it
does smell truly foetid. Past the hamlet, the land on the left-hand side
rises and, as the road sweeps along towards a distant bend, the limestone
of the hill shows significant red/brown staining where a short-cut route
has been worn.

Taking this short-cut is rewarding in many ways – not least
floristically. For those not familiar with weathering of limestone, this
area provides a good example. The weird knobbly shapes of some of the

rocks seem to be mimicked and expanded by a dark purplish-green
holly-leaved shrub. Quite often these contorted mounds have bright red,
shining, berry-like structures, which are in fact oak apples – this being
the holly oak from which ancient civilizations obtained a scarlet dye.
Here these 'trees' are goat or sheep blasted; they are so heavily grazed
that they never reach tree-like proportions. Amongst these purplish
mounds may be found **Orchis papillionacea** and also **Orchis
quadripunctata**: **Fritillaria messanensis**. is also recorded from this
area. The shelter provided by hollows in the limestone is often enough
for them to be colonised by **Cyclamen creticum** or **Arisarum vulgare.**

**Orchis papillionacea
(about twice life-size)**

Orchis papillionacea with holly oak leaves above

Arisarum vulgare in a limestone hollow

Rejoining the road, the next feature to look for, almost immediately
on the right, is an ancient paved donkey-path (kalderimi) that is in fact
quite wide (certainly two-way, though not dual carriageway). Following
this kalderimi quickly brings one to the Aradena Gorge – and, for some
people, a gasp! Probably this is a spot for refreshment, photography, and

The kalderimi in the gorge at Aradena

Aradena church viewed from across the gorge

a little contemplation. Here one would have to be grossly insensitive not to be impressed with some sense of history, and respect for previous civilisations.

The kalderimi in the gorge is, for the most part, well preserved, and has angled ridges to deflect surface water outwards. The south side of the gorge is particularly favoured by **Gagea graeca**. Further down on the south side the Cretan endemic shrub **Staehelina petiolata** overhangs the path with **Ptilostemon chamaepeuce**. When the path approaches the gorge floor, on the right-hand side may be found **Cyclamen creticum**, and **Symphytum creticum**, a rather exotic-looking member of the Boraginaceae. The kalderimi on the north side of the gorge has a cave behind it, just above the gorge floor. **Verbascum arcturus** hangs precariously from its ceiling. The north side is usually a hot ascent, and at the top, under the shade of trees, is an ideal spot for a picnic lunch: a picnic table has recently been provided for the purpose.

Bridge over the Aradena Gorge

The path leads to the group of houses that constituted the centre of Aradena, a sad and virtually abandoned village. Recently some of the buildings are being renovated, mercifully in a very sympathetic way. It's certainly worth having a close look at the old church, though unfortunately it is kept locked. From the church it's a short walk to the bridge (made in the UK) back over the gorge.

The bridge, or its ends, provide a good vantage point for viewing the geological spectacle; and watching birds of prey patrolling, or a hoopoe crossing the gorge.

Returning via the road towards Anopoli, there is quite soon a vehicular track to the right. We take and follow this through a rather grey 'lunar' limestone landscape. There is eventually a green area that relieves the eye: it is a small 'doline', a basin-shaped area in the limestone (which has probably been dissolved by rainfall and then underground drainage), that has partially filled with soil, to the extent that here it is cultivated.

The small doline by the track from Aradena to Livaniana

Further along the track the backdrop of the Levka Ori is lost behind a near horizon; soon after that, the view is in front of us, as we come over the horizon to a coastal seascape.

Coastal view, with the Aradena Gorge and Livaniana

The track is now a recent zigzag scar on a south facing slope. Soon after the westernmost bend, there is a way-marked route – one could hardly call it a path – that soon joins the ancient path which leads to Livaniana. This path makes progress much more interesting, especially when it turns right, into a cleft between rocks through which St. Athanasius' church can be seen as part of the panoramic view of the top of the lower section of the Aradena Gorge.

Steps take us down to an area where the coloured banding of the rocks deserves more than a passing glance.

The path now leads us between fields, the walls of which are topped with wire netting, and emerges on to the path just above Livaniana's church.

'Surprise view' of the church of St. Athanasius

Last view of the Aradena Gorge

This is now probably familiar territory for those who have walked to Livaniana before. Retracing the route to Phoenix and Loutro, probably after a break at the taverna, should prove no problem, though the views are different and the lighting conditions can add a magical touch. Sheep, some with bells, returning to the fold in the long shadows of a low sun may be the reward of a late return.

The path to Phoenix goes quite close to the beach, which can be very inviting for a swim after a long walk – though one needs to take care, since there are reports of spiny echinoderms around the rocky sides. These relatives of starfish, look like pin-cushions (often black), and if trodden on, the spines break off, causing painful multiple wounds. Lightweight plastic shoes provide good protection.

Another treat, if the weather is good, is to be by the castle at Loutro as the sun sets, and see Mount Ida in a pink glow.

An alternative route home from Livaniana is to follow way-marks down to Likkos Bay, with its selection of tavernas, and then follow the E4 back to Loutro.

6. Half-day walk: Paleohora and its 'mountain'

Paleohora is a place that lacks immediate appeal for many people; however, stop for a week, and it's highly probable you will return.

The jetty at Paleohora

This first walk starts at the southernmost point of the Paleohora peninsula, and to get there from the jetty on the eastern side of town one will be passing by some of the oldest inhabited buildings of Paleohora. In Spring many will have tended flowers: by the time the Aris Hotel is reached, one knows that scented white lilies grow well here.

From the road that loops around the peninsula tip, take the turning northwards up towards the coastguards' lookout. As soon as the bend in the road straightens out on top of the 'plateau', look for a palm tree on the right hand side. It is **Phoenix theophrasti**, once thought to be a Cretan endemic but now known to be found at a few other locations. It

**View of Paleohora from the sea: this walk starts from the
greenery at the left, and finishes on the right hand skyline
'mountain'**

can be easily distinguished from the oft planted **Phoenix canariensis**,
which has relatively soft leaflets, as **P. theophrasti** leaflets may be sharp
and tough enough to draw blood! This species was thought to have been
identical to the date palm, but now is recognised as distinct; its fruits are
quite different from dates.

We walk past the coastguards' lookout, and across the small plateau
area to the site of the Venetian castle at the northern end. It is being
excavated; no easy task given the site's long, chequered and violent
history: though the renovations have already given the area more of a
feeling of significance. But it is the views that impress most people.

To the west is a picture-postcard view of the extensive sandy beach,
with behind it the local 'mountains', which have sprouted three
communications aerials. Further to the west is the Koundoura Peninsula,
destination for another walk (see no.9), and beyond that, the last
headland is Akrotiri Krios.

View over Paleohora from the Venetian castle

To the east the view encompasses more of the town's rooftops, and beyond, a succession of headlands and mountains fade into the haze; there may still be crisp snow on the visible Levka Ori peaks.

Moving down the steps from the castle soon brings us past the town's church, with its very recently built bell-tower. This is the major focus of the town at Easter. Immediately below the church the street-sides usually have a colourful display of flowers including lilies, delphiniums and nasturtiums, underneath the whitewashed trunks of white mulberry trees whose branches above are pruned and trained.

A picnic lunch can be quickly bought, and then our walk continues through the town towards the sandy beach (westwards). Turning right by a skyline date-palm and walking along the road at the back of the beach we pass some eye-catching displays: not only oleanders and the wonderfully scented **Pittosporum tobira**, but also frangipani and bougainvillea. One of the gardens also has a mature loquat tree, which looks very exotic with its large dark green leaves contrasting with the small, light-apricot-coloured fruits (which are very refreshing – they are

Paleohora street with nasturtiums, lilies and white mulberry

sold locally). Soon after there is a left-hand bend and a slight upward gradient, and a turning to the right to Voutas. Follow this road briefly to the new estate housing for Paleohora residents, take a right turning, and beyond the eastern edge of the development walk upwards, and then through a wire fence 'gate'.

The sides of this, now partially concreted, track are not hugely floriferous, but sometimes there is a good display of **Bubonium aquaticum**; and further up the track, on a part which is sheltered and south facing, the Cretan endemic **Centaurea idaea** flowers early in the season.

If you are beginning to doubt the wisdom of walking up a mountain (albeit a small one) in the late morning, probably in full sun, then relief is soon at hand, as you reach a saddle area and walk down into an olive grove and some shade. If you haven't already been impressed by **Dracunculus vulgaris** flowers (illustrated on pages 5 and 138), then probably it will happen here.

Bubonium aquaticum; Nerium oleander in the background

As we follow the track towards the eastern radio mast, in the open country the vegetation is dominated by the rather dull coloured **Sarcopoterium spinosum** (looking a bit like wire netting) and many low, grey, spiny, but not yet flowering **Coridothymus capitatus** bushes, which release wonderful aromatics when trodden on. The distinctive apricot-yellow flowers of **Fumana arabica**, and the more vibrant yellow of the smaller **Fumana thymifolia**, often provide colour and movement – fluttering in the slightest breeze to attract insects. Wonderful contrast is provided by early pink flowers of **Cistus creticus**;

Centaurea idaea (Cretan endemic)

Olive grove in the saddle area of Paleohora's mountain

and to underline the geological fact that we are on limestone, a few **Anacamptis pyramidalis** (pyramid orchid) spikes may be in flower. If it's past noon there may be many small flowers – from palest powder, to intense royal blue – of **Gynandriris sisyrinchium** scattered over patches of bare ground. Their blooming is very brief; each flower opening after mid-day, and then only lasting till dusk.

Gynandriris sisyrinchium (possibly G. monophylla)

At the peak, just beyond the mast, the view is wonderful. Paleohora below appears rather like a map; but in the east and north the very mountainous nature of the area and its emptiness are what impresses.

This may be the place to enjoy one's picnic lunch, or alternatively retrace steps to sea level and picnic on a beach; the sandy town beach is closest, but there are quieter pebbly ones further along the Koundoura road to the west.

**View of Paleohora; jetty on the east side,
sandy beach to the west**

View to the east; the first low promontory is a Gialiskari Beach

7. Paleohora to Anidri and Gialiskari Beaches

The route out of Paleohora for this walk starts at the Livikon Hotel building where a road branches east from the main Hania road. At the next T-junction turn left and follow the road out past the cemetery.

Chrysanthemum coronarium by the road to Anidri

The road through the olive groves may be bordered with **Galactites tomentosa**, and this is an area where the double form of the invasive weed **Oxalis pes-caprae** is found. The road passes 'Camping Paleohora', soon after which there are large specimens of **Opuntia ficus-barbarica** ('Prickly pear', an introduction from the New World, brought to Europe by Christopher Columbus). On the right-hand side may be a border of **Chrysanthemum coronarium** between the road and the beach. Immediately after a left-hand bend there is a turning to the right that descends to a bridge: this is our return route.

The main road continues, but now uphill. Once some height has been reached it is interesting to look at the colour pattern of trees and shrubs in the right-hand side-valley. The predominant colour is a dark green or grey green, – in places enlivened by bursts of yellow **Calicotome villosa** flowers (a very gorse-like shrub): but the bottom of the river valley is mostly clothed in the light fresh green leaves of **Platanus orientalis** (a parent of the London plane), a deciduous tree that favours areas where its roots can be near the water table. In places the roadside weeds are dominated by **Notobasis syriaca**, a rather elegant and distinguished thistle, and in other areas are many handsome specimens of **Verbascum macrurum**.

As the road turns right over a bridge, it is worth pausing to look on the right-hand side at the flowers growing on a boulder. **Gagea graeca** is here (the Greek lily) along with an **Allium sp**. whose flowers are similar but with more pointed petals, and lacking the graceful funnel shape of the gagea. Of course, on bruising, an **Allium sp**. will smell of onions.

On the bank a few metres further on, along with the nearly ubiquitous grey-leaved 'garden centre plant' **Ballota pseudodictamnus**, grows **Bryonia cretica** and also **Mandragora autumnalis** ('Mandrake'). The plant, whose roots look like a man, is reputed to shriek if pulled from the ground. Mandrake was used as an anaesthetic, often with other drugs, from Pliny's time (1st century AD) until the middle of the 19th century when ether was first used.

The road now leads through a minor gorge where several chasmophytes can reliably be seen. On the left-hand side there are many plants of **Ebenus cretica** and **Petromarula pinnata**, whilst the right-hand wall has **Verbascum arcturus** and **Ptilostemon chamaepeuce**. As the gorge opens out, **Cyclamen creticum** may be found, and further on the orchids **Anacamptis pyramidalis**, **Ophrys sphegodes subsp. gortynia**, and **Orchis italica**. We are now walking through a lush area

71

Bryonia cretica

Mandragora autumnalis

of olive groves and floriferous meadows studded with the vibrant blue
Muscari comosum.

At a significant bend in the road to the left, keep straight on along a
small path into the olive grove. It may not be much of a short cut in terms
of distance; but immediately one is under dappled shade, with more
varied ground than asphalt to tread on. I was leading a group through a
grassy clearing here one Spring, when swallows decided to swoop and
weave between the members of our party: a magical happening.

The path rejoins the asphalt road just before it enters the village
of Anidri, with garden roses and the scented hanging trumpets of
Brugmansia suaveolens by way of greeting. Before taking some
refreshment at the taverna (which is a converted school house), the
ancient olive tree on the opposite side of the road is worth more than a
glance. Stone seats placed amongst its gnarled roots are still partially
visible even after the recent road surfacing.

To visit the village church (as opposed to the hilltop church), take the
south-west path from the taverna between houses and then downhill to
the right. The church is usually open. It has extensive frescoes (partially
obliterated) and the unusual feature of two altars.

Continuing to follow the path downwards, there is a junction at which
we bear to the right towards a hill to the south, which is topped by
another church. The path eventually turns to the left, following a terrace
and then zigzagging up the hill. Even if hot and tired, one's eyes may
spot **Ophrys holoserica**, **Ophrys lutea**, and – usually earlier in the
season – **Orchis quadripunctata** by the path. The church at the summit,
where there is often a good display of **Phlomis fruticosa**, is simple
and bare, and mainly notable for its separate bell-hanging, but the view
is quite special: both back over the village of Anidri with the road
snaking towards Prodromi, and to the south over the mini-gorge that
ends at the three Gialiskari Beaches. Their name refers to their facing
approximately south-east, south and south-west, so one of them is likely
to be a 'smooth harbour'.

Retracing steps down from the church, you soon come to delightful
picnic areas. The vegetation on which you sit is aromatic with **Lagoecia
cuminoides**, and the browning leaves and fruit of tulips suggest what it
must have been like a month earlier. By the end of April you need to be
high in the Levka Ori to see tulips in flower (see Walk 10).

The return to the bottom of the hill takes us into the olive grove where
there is a junction, and a now concreted track to the right is our route to

Our path through the dappled shade of an olive grove

**Old olive tree with seating stones, opposite the former school
house (now a taverna) in Anidri**

the gorge. Following signs to the beach, take the path into the gorge
floor, which is our way down to the sea.

Do remember to stop and look up occasionally: this is only a mini-
gorge by Cretan standards, but one can still feel quite dwarfed by the
surroundings.

At one point, the way down is via a curved, smooth water-shoot worn
into the limestone (dry in Spring!). This may appear forbidding at first
sight, but it is no obstacle to the moderately able bodied, and it seems
thoroughly appropriate that sliding down on one's backside further
smooths the rocks.

The walls of the gorge support chasmophytes, and here I have found
small quantities of **Origanum dictamnus** clinging closely adpressed to
the rocks, their oppositely-arranged, softly downy, triangular leaves
looking very tactile. This is the plant that traditionally is used as an
infusion for local 'mountain tea'.

Within this gorge you may be lucky enough to see the flowers of
Convolvulus oleifolius, and also the aptly named **C. elegantissimus**.

Phlomis fruticosa near Anidri hill church

Lunch stop above Anidri

Origanum dictamnus (Cretan endemic), photographed in Autumn

Convolvulus oleifolius

The gorge ends at the Gialiskari Beaches where I highly recommend you take a break. The bay to the south-east usually has gravel or coarse sand as an easy entrance to the water for swimming; the south bay is pebbles, and the west bay is a mixture: but it may be the wind and waves that determine where you sit or swim.

To return to Paleohora follow the car track from the car park upwards and westwards (there is not a path at sea level). This track has virtually no shade and one is walking into the sun. It is often a stark contrast of sandy grey path and shimmering light on the water: an experience I appreciate more in the cool of the evening.

You eventually join the Anidri road of our outward journey. The way home is virtually on the level, passing the cemetery (which may now be dimly illuminated with candles), as you enter Paleohora.

Gialiskari Beach, looking east

8. Paleohora to Rodovani, Strati, Azogires, and Anidri

This is a very long walk: in its longest form, from dawn to dusk.

When first planned, it was mostly on rough tracks with a little asphalt: now it is mostly asphalt, with a little rough path. The great diversity of countryside walked through is still the same.

This 'walk' starts by catching the early bus (about dawn) to Rodovani. Its normal stopping place is in the village, but it may drop you at the T-junction with the road to Souyia. Here you can see the valley going down towards Souyia, and upwards to the Levka Ori. Walking back into the village, with the bus gone, it is probably very quiet, maybe the odd sheep being milked, but little besides to disturb the peace.

Early morning in the lush area around Maza

Beyond the village you will probably notice a distinctive smell as you tread on, or brush against **Dittrichia viscosa** (stinking inula), a common roadside weed here, which has small yellow flowers later in the year. At one of the many bends in the road there will probably be a display of blue flowers of **Lupinus pilosus** (whose seeds are often used as human food). This is an area of lushness, with many trees, possibly golden orioles calling, and a varied roadside flora including **Orchis collina, Serapias sp., Ranunculus asiaticus** (white, pink and red forms), **Orchis simia**; and oranges growing in the hamlet of Maza.

Orchis simia

81

Ranunculus asiaticus

Around Maza a variety of species of oaks grow, and there may be a colourful display of lupins with the striking yellow-green (euphorbia-like) foliage of **Smyrnium perfoliatum** as roadside weeds. Beyond the church on the left, the countryside soon becomes more open and rather barren, though the roadside 'weed' of **Cistus salviifolius** would hardly be out of place at the Chelsea flower show!

Cistus salviifolius

As the road approaches Temenia the 'moorland' impression wanes and the amount of **Smyrnium perfoliatum** increases.

Instead of just following the road to Paleohora at a T junction, a brief diversion up the right-hand road (towards Kandanos and Hania) for a few hundred metres brings one to a bottling factory for Temenion, a local soft-drinks brand name. It is situated in such a sensible location: by a spring, in an area where citrus fruits grow, and at a route junction.

Returning to, and following along, the road to Paleohora, we find that the countryside becomes more open and rather barren as it rises, though roadside colour is still with us.

Smyrnium perfoliatum in the foreground, Vicia villosa subsp. varia and Papaver rhoeas behind

Tragopogon sinuatus (showing a variety of form)

Hypericum empetrifolium (approx. life-size)

As the road reaches its highest point there are expansive views down towards Paleohora, and the view of the Levka Ori peaks is lost. When the road bends sharply to the right, at its summit, there is soon a short track on the right-hand side by a cultivated field. Take this short track to the rough ground behind: then walk carefully because there are so many orchids and other interesting plants here, that it's difficult to know where to put one's feet. I remember a walker in one of my groups, whose constant theme had been the superior floral displays in Corsica, spontaneously exclaiming, "This is better than Corsica!"

The plants below (not a complete floral list; more a list of the obvious and the easily identified) are from an area probably less than 50 metres by 50 metres (2,500 square metres).

Aceras anthropophorum, Asphodeline lutea, Asphodelus aestivus, Briza maxima, Calicotome villosa, Cephalanthera longifolia, Cistus creticus, C. salviifolius, Cytinus hypocistis, Erica arborea, Gagea graeca, Hypericum empetrifolium, Ophrys fleischmannii, O. heldreichii, O. lutea, O. sphegodes subsp. gortynia, O. spruneri, Orchis anatolica, O. collina, O. coriophora subsp. fragrans, O. italica, O. papillionacea, O. pauciflora, O. quadripunctata, O. simia, Polygala venulosa, Sarcopoterium spinosum, Serapias sp., Trifolium stellatum, Tuberaria guttata, Vicia parviflora, Vicia villosa subsp. varia.

I find it easy to lose track of time whilst botanising here: it's usually someone else's pangs of hunger that cause us to leave.

The snowy skyline is lost as we descend around a bend in the road where there may be a honey-like scent in the air from **Erica arborea** flowering on both sides of the road, accompanied by the bright green bushes of **Arbutus unedo** (the strawberry tree). Further along, on the right hand side, there is a **Cydonia oblonga** (quince tree), presumably planted, which has very distinguished flowers.

Asphodelus aestivus and Calicotome villosa are the most obvious flowers; many orchids grow between them

Cytinus hypocistis (buds), growing on Cistus salviifolius

Ophrys fleischmannii

88

Ophrys spruneri (approx. twice life-size)

Orchis pauciflora and Orchis quadripunctata

Trifolium stellatum, Orchis quadripunctata, Ophrys lutea and Gagea graeca

Polygala venulosa

Tuberaria guttata

91

Cephalanthera longifolia

Ranunculus sp.

Levka Ori viewed from the floristically rich site near Strati

Cydonia oblonga

94

Serapias sp.   **Orchis laxiflora**

By a cistern, presumably surrounded by damp soil for many years, there may be a show of **Serapias** flowers, with **Orchis laxiflora** amongst the **Juncus effusus**.

We are now in Strati. After a church high up a bank on the right, the road-verges may be blue with **Lupinus pilosus**, growing with **Iris albicans** whose ivory-white flowers provide an aesthetic contrast. Just before a hairpin bend that takes the road onto the opposite side of the valley, the wayside vegetation can be very colourful, when **Calicotome villosa** and **Vicia villosa** are flowering together.

A track that leads upwards from the road soon after the bend provides a good picnic spot, being sheltered from winds, having an olive tree for shade and a host of flowers.

Calicotome villosa, Vicia villosa and Asphodelus aestivus

Orchis anatolica

Arum cyrenaicum

97

Cistus salviifolius, Calicotome villosa, Asphodelus aestivus and Orchis anatolica

From here the road leads mostly downwards towards Paleohora, but undertaking many meandering loops as it goes. We pass the village washing-facility on our right, and many floral treats by the roadsides.

Eventually the road is near the valley floor, and delightfully – and unusually for Crete – we are accompanied not only by occasional shade from olive or plane trees, but also the sound of running water. There is a left turning off the road, which we would ignore except that the stream is forded by the side track, and there is a small waterfall. Given this spot of shade and cool, it is usual to pause awhile.

The hamlet of Azogires is not much further down the valley, and has two establishments that provide refreshment. Some people may decide to terminate their walk here: though a taxi or other vehicular means of getting back is best arranged the day before.

For walking enthusiasts there is the relief of finding that the continuation of the walk to Anidri quickly takes us off asphalt at the first left turning downhill in Azogires. It is probably signed 'To the Museum'. The path winds down to the stream's course where there was once a mill. Beyond this it skirts an abandoned monastery, in part of which the museum is housed. The path becomes rather overgrown in places, but there are way-marks. The peace and quiet and panoramic views over Azogires and the valley are wonderful. This is a good place to observe the 'painting by numbers' effect given by light-green **Platanus orientalis** following the water courses, darker grey-green of olive trees filling in most of the lower gaps, some slightly brighter (at this time of year) green **Quercus coccifera** (holly oak) tree-patches, generally higher up the valley sides, abutting yellow patches of flowering **Calicotome villosa**, which give way to grey rocky areas above. In several areas the **Quercus coccifera** has grown free of grazing and provides shade under which one may find **Cyclamen creticum** flowering. In more open areas **Cistus creticus** is a colourful companion. The path eventually leads slightly eastwards and down into Anidri. This is the place that is usually the walk's end – transport back to Paleohora having been arranged the previous day.

For those with considerable amounts of fortitude, the walk back to Paleohora from Anidri may have its rewards. By now it's likely to be near sunset, but once I certainly had enough light to watch a barn owl in the gorge section; and bats will probably be one's 'company' further along the road.

The lights of Paleohora may feel *very* welcoming.

9. Paleohora to the Koundoura Peninsula

This is a short and easy walk: a relative rest day.

Take the way out of Paleohora described in walk 6, until the turning off for Voutas which, on this walk, we ignore, continuing westwards. The road is straight, and unfortunately locals tend to use it as a racetrack; but whilst walking on the verges, especially on the seaward side, aniseed smell from **Foeniculum vulgare** (fennel) may be a pleasant distraction; on the landward side the flat areas behind the fence are sometimes carpeted with blue, white and yellow dots of **Solenopsis minuta** flowers.

When the land on the right hand side of the road rises, it is worth inspecting. Here is very clear evidence of a raised beach, the former water lap-line is very obvious, and above are what were probably cave entrances, one with a striking (so early!) example of a gothic arch. These are reminders that this is an area of relatively recent, dramatic geological

Raised beach with caves above

Onopordum illyricum

uplift; the present-day sea level being several metres lower than the elevated lap-line.

Beyond this the roadsides often have growing on them the huge and vicious looking thistle **Onopordum illyricum**.

We then cross two new bridges in quick succession (one of the old ones was swept away, and the other severely damaged, in the deluge of Spring 2000). The road moves inland slightly and very soon afterwards we take a track on the left, southwards, to the Koundoura peninsula. After passing a few plastic greenhouses, probably containing tomatoes,

**View eastwards towards Paleohora from the Koundoura
Peninsula**

we reach an isthmus area, where the sea can be seen on both sides of the
peninsula.

Keeping to the east we make our way between rocks and small sand
dunes, still southwards. The major plants acting as sand-dune formers
here are **Cupressus sempervirens** (the wild 'type' form of the Italian
cypress), and **Juniperus oxycedrus macrocarpa**, a relatively
uncommon juniper.

At the southernmost point there is a rocky and open sandy area where
salt panning occurs on a small scale, there being a very restricted access
of sea water (through a cave on the western side of the peninsula tip).

On the western side, leading back into the shrubby area, there are
usually many cheerful mauve and yellow flowers of **Malcolmia sp.**, and
the pink flowers of **Silene colorata**; and quite often one will disturb a
small flock of heron which slowly flap away.

When you reach the sandy beach, before establishing yourself for a
picnic, do look at the open space's vegetation, which consists largely of
two species: (1) the daffodil-like leaves of **Pancratium maritimum**
(which is indeed called the 'Sea Daffodil', and is scented, white and

Near the southern point of the Koundoura Peninsula

Silene colorata

beautiful, but flowers in late summertime); (2) **Centaurea pumilio**, a low-growing, purple-to-whitish-flowered thistle-like plant which is actually rare; though here it is locally very abundant (but not to be sat on – for more than one reason).

You return to Paleohora by retracing your steps. The journey takes about an hour; useful to know if one is tempted to watch the sun go down from the beach.

The Samaria Gorge and Gingilos Mountain walks

The Samaria Gorge from the path to Gingilos Mountain

These walks can only be undertaken on successive days after the 1st. of May when the Samara Gorge is fully open: an overnight stop at Omalos is very highly recommended. The path to Linoseli Col (Walk 10) takes one above snow patches and early Spring flowers such as crocus and chionodoxa, to a view that, on a clear day, encompasses both the South and North coasts of Crete. The summit of Gingilos at 2080m has a splendid 'alpine' feel about it, although several of the flowers there are Cretan endemics. The following day's walk (no. 11) is down the famous Samaria Gorge (Europe's longest), seeing cyclamen and peonies en route to the sea, where temperatures may entice one to swim before taking the scenically dramatic boat-trip back to either Hora Sfakion or Paleohora.

Most people, when visiting the Samaria Gorge, make a very early morning start that gives the event a sense of dramatic occasion. Those

Dawn over the Levka Ori

approaching from the West in Spring may see the sun rising over the Levka Ori mountains as they pass through small villages. The journey from Paleohora passes through obviously different vegetation types which are associated with elevation, rainfall and soil type. Away from limestone the natives **Erica arborea** and **Arbutus unedo** flourish, and where sufficiently moist in these areas, chestnut-groves (of **Castanea sativa** – sweet chestnut) have been planted. Above this the vegetation is rather sparse, but the views become increasingly dramatic to both north and south coasts, as the road follows the summit of an east-west watershed ridge, before descending onto the Omalos Plain (a large doline).

As the road leaves the plain to reach the upper access point to the Samaria Gorge (Xiloskala), there are specimens of the small twiggy tree **Zelkova abelicea** (not only a Cretan endemic but a legally protected vulnerable species) growing on its south-western banks. (The leaves of **Zelkova** are small, significantly longer than broad, and are coarsely serrated: there is a specimen planted in the grounds of the Neos Omalos Hotel.)

10. Xiloskala to Linoseli Col, Gingilos Mountain and Omalos

From the very welcoming restaurant, the road leads upwards for one hairpin bend and then stops in front of steps from which the path to Linoseli Col and Gingilos is signposted to the right. This route is a seemingly endless, zigzagging, rough-surfaced path that does have the merit of gaining altitude quickly. Spring flowers that will distract you are those of the 4-petalled pink/purple **Aubrietia deltoidea** (a common plant of English gardens), and cheerful white clusters of **Cerastium scaposum** (a Cretan endemic) usually quivering in a breeze.

Cerastium scaposum (Cretan endemic)

107

Aethionema saxatile

A much more substantial and striking plant that also grows in this area is **Aethionema saxatile**.

Near the top of this section the view of the Omalos Plain becomes very impressive, but once the path levels off, you are in the catchment of the Samaria and the view is dominated by the plunging face of Gingilos. If you take time to rest, then be sure not to sit on 'cushions' of vegetation: **Berberis cretica** is very common in this area, and is very spiny!

It is at about this altitude that the arresting vivid blue flowers of **Anchusa caespitosa** (a Cretan endemic, the colour of **Gentiana verna**) will be seen. Once the eye has been attracted by the colour, the plant's form may strike one as interesting, all parts being closely adpressed to the ground as a survival strategy against grazing.

Cupressus sempervirens and Gingilos base; early morning

109

Anchusa caespitosa (Cretan endemic, approx. twice life-size)

The path now becomes easier both in surface and gradient, and is even, in parts, descending. However, progress may often be interrupted by the need to stand and stare. A both inspiring and daunting prospect is that the first destination of Linoseli Col is now in sight on the skyline.

There is quite a long stretch downwards to a rock arch, beyond which the terrain is awesome. The silence can be so intense that one's own heartbeat and breathing seem intrusive. Occasionally there is birdsong; and alpine choughs calling in quick succession sometimes indicate the presence of an eagle in the vicinity.

Soon after the arch, the path leads upwards again and the vegetation becomes sparse, with only a few mature trees.

Not far above the tree line a stream emerges, and at least provides an opportunity to refill one's water bottle, if not pause for a longer rest before the trek to the Col.

Walkers heading towards the arch, Linoseli Col on the skyline

Path through the rock arch

**A sense of scale is not always easy to maintain in this area
(our path under a Cupressus sempervirens tree)**

**Cupressus sempervirens and Acer sempervirens
below Linoseli Col**

**Ranunculus sp. and the Cretan endemic Scilla nana
(one of the chionodoxas) by the spring**

114

The onward path is often less distinct than before, over rather loose scree, but after many zigzags the path improves before reaching the Col. In sheltered nooks and crannies where there is stable rock and soil, **Scilla nana** (chionodoxa) and **Crocus sieberi** may still be in flower.

Scilla nana (chionodoxa) and Crocus sieberi (both Cretan endemics) overhung by spines of Berberis cretica.

Be careful when approaching the top of the Col, since often the Northern side (our approach) is sheltered, whereas at the rim the wind can be blowing with enough force to blow an adult over. Open jackets must be secured so that they do not act as a sail!

Once over the Col rim, it comes as something of a surprise to find that its Southern slopes are quite green with vegetation, unlike the virtually barren Northern scree. If you rest here, choose your spot for sitting with care, for not only is there **Berberis cretica** to avoid (which is fairly obviously spiny), but also **Astragalus sps**. which *look* like soft cushions of moss, but are more akin to pin cushions and can certainly draw blood. Another reason for taking care in this area is that one may inadvertently crush a **Tulipa cretica**.

Tulipa cretica (Cretan endemic, approx. twice life-size)

Always a small plant, **Tulipa cretica** (a Cretan endemic) in these exposed situations at high altitude seldom exceeds 2cm in height, and unless the flowers are open enough to expose the yellow stigma, anthers and internal throat, they are easily overlooked. Once you have seen one, you usually begin to notice more; the open flowers varying from white to rose.

Flowers much more easily spotted are those of another Cretan endemic, **Viola fragrans**. The blooms are borne on relatively long and slender stalks, with the result that their movement, in even slight breezes, makes them more noticeable (to pollinating insects as well as humans).

Very much more static are the flowers of **Prunus prostrata**, a shrub that often forms mounds closely moulded against rocks.

Further up the way-marked path from Linoseli Col towards Gingilos, the going soon becomes more of a scramble; and can be very taxing for vertigo sufferers. Between sections of bare rock the path is usually obvious and often made cheerful by tulips; and violets and aubrieta which stay with us until the summit. If you examine the ground flora closely you will probably spot the minute blue flowers of **Cynoglossum sphacioticum**, a Cretan endemic found only on the Levka Ori. Approaching the first summit the path becomes much easier and the panoramic view more impressive.

It very much depends on the snow cover as to how many and where one sees **Crocus sieberi subsp. sieberi** (yet another Cretan endemic). This seems very much a 'snow melt' species, being extremely ephemeral after snow.

The sense of achievement gained through having reached the first summit is considerable. The view to the south coast testifies to the very steep gradients from sea level to Gingilos; the view to the north coast, often lost in haze, is impressive, as are the peaks to the east. If weather conditions are such that these are not visible, then perhaps one should not be staying too long.

Viola fragrans (Cretan endemic, approx. twice life-size)

Prunus prostrata

Cynoglossum sphacioticum
(Cretan endemic, approx. twice life-size)

Aubrieta deltoidea with Tulipa cretica

Cairn at the first summit of Gingilos

Crocus sieberi subsp. sieberi at the summit of Gingilos

121

Crocus sieberi subsp. sieberi (Cretan endemic)

Snow melt flowers at summit of Gingilos

The author at Gingilos' highest peak

If conditions are good then it is a relatively easy walk / scramble to the highest peak of Gingilos, though in places it's a matter of following way-marks across very chunky blocks of rock. The view from this second peak is more restricted to the south, but dramatic looking towards Omalos; and the feel is one of finality.

The journey down is not such an anticlimax as you might imagine. Yes, it is retracing steps, but perspectives are very different and instead of being faced with a rising horizon that is foreground; your sightlines are more often the panoramic vistas, not to mention the changing lighting conditions that enhance them. Great care should, however, be taken on the descent; after the euphoria of reaching the summit, it is only too easy to relax into complacency and miss your footing.

Walking down from Gingilos towards Linoseli Col

Rocky path from Linoseli Col

Approaching the arch on the path from Linoseli Col

Cupressus sempervirens and Gingilos base; late afternoon

A striking view that could cause dismay is of the Omalos Plain from above. If staying the night at Omalos then to see your destination at the far end of a long, straight, flat road is not inspiring. However, arrangements can usually be made to be picked up from the Xiloskala restaurant.

The Omalos Plain doline, viewed from the path to Xiloskala

Whether you have a weary trudge, or are whisked across the Omalos Plain in a truck or minibus, do keep your natural history faculties alert. There are usually flowers of **Anemone coronaria** dotted here and there, and if you pay particular attention to fenced-off areas from which sheep and goats have been excluded you may spot drifts of **Tulipa saxatilis**.

Tulipa saxatilis is a variable species, some authorities recognising the variant **T. bakeri** as a separate species. It seems that there is probably gene flow from the **T. bakeri** types to **T. saxatilis** at high altitudes; and from **T. cretica** to **T. saxatilis** at lower altitudes. Even the casual

Sheep grazing on the Omalos Plain

observer of tulips at Omalos will notice variations of flower shape, as well as colour and markings.

The sheep and goats are quite likely to be on the move during the evening (being brought into pens for milking) so that progress of vehicles along the road is, at least at times, reduced to a good plant-spotting crawl. If you are unlucky enough not to find tulips in flower on a walk out of Omalos village, the pastoral scene of sheep being milked is probably a reasonable consolation prize.

Tulipa saxatilis on the Omalos Plain

11. Omalos to Samaria Gorge, Agia Roumeli and Paleohora

The civilized way to start this walk is after having spent the night at Omalos. In this way one can arrive at Xiloskala (the wooden steps) early in the morning, fresh from a good night's sleep and having recently had a good breakfast; and, hopefully before too many coaches arrive.

Tickets are purchased at the entrance, and the steps downward begin immediately. The gorge is long (the longest in Europe), spectacular in several places, and in Spring the flowers are a delight; it is no wonder that it is a major tourist attraction and thus entry is restricted, the gorge is patrolled and there is a rescue service.

The 'wooden steps', as shown in the picture, are the means of descending in zigzag fashion, down the side of the gorge to the riverbed.

Quite soon after entering the gorge, flowers catch the eye, for example those of **Onosma erectum** growing out of the gorge walls.

It's usually not long before one notices the leaves of cyclamen with their distinctive pink / purple undersides; and then a few white flowers.

These are some of the distractions that help one forget the strain on muscles in a continuous descent; but the lightness that one experiences on 'gliding' up the small incline from the riverbed has to be experienced to be believed!

Soon after reaching the riverbed there are areas which are carpeted with cyclamen flowers – a good reason in itself to 'walk the Samaria'.

On the way down, the views between the trees – mainly **Cupressus sempervirens** and **Pinus brutia** – are spectacular towards Linoseli Col. After one has been walking for quite some time, it is interesting to note that the glimpses of the face of Gingilos have changed very little. Progress down the gorge has been more or less vertical to the point where one at last reaches the riverbed. The temperature usually rises, during the descent, partly due to the rising sun, but also the decreasing altitude and increasing shelter.

The aromatic smells of Cupressus and Pinus are soon joined by those of **Cistus creticus**.

Part of the rescue service of the Samaria Gorge at Xiloskala

Onosma erectum

Cyclamen creticum (Cretan endemic)

Cistus creticus

Not all the flowers are as showy and obvious as **Cistus creticus**; in dappled shade one may spot the restrained tones of **Fritillaria messanensis**.

One of the many delights of walking the Samaria Gorge is the way it springs surprises. Just as it seems that the wooden steps will never end, they do in a small clearing at the riverbed; it is refreshing to be walking with the sound of trickling or rushing water; and then there is calm and silence when it disappears underground; one gets used to walking under trees and then there is suddenly a burst of clear light as at the glade of Agios Nikolaos.

Here the sparkling display of ground cover flowers is given by **Asphodelus aestivus**, with a few blotches of the deep dark red of **Dracunculus vulgaris**.

Fritillaria messanensis

Also at Agios Nikolaos, one can reliably find **Paeonia clusii**, a showy Cretan endemic, that would be difficult for plant breeders to improve upon, both in visual proportions and scent.

The arresting but foul-smelling flowers of **Dracunculus vulgaris** are quite commonly found in Spring, from here to sea level.

Further along, in an area much more heavily shaded by trees, but very close to the path, in some years one may be lucky enough to see the flowers of **Limodorum abortivum**. This is a rare orchid, which is saprophytic (gains nourishment from dead organic material), and its leaves are reduced to scales clasping the stem.

Pool in the Samaria river

Glade at Agios Nikolaos

Paeonia clusii (Cretan endemic, approx. one half life-size)

Dracunculus vulgaris

Looking down the Samaria Gorge

Limodorum abortivum (approx. life-size)

Another orchid, which is much more common and quite likely to be seen, though in sunnier spots, is **Ophrys heldreichii**.

A much larger and showier plant **Verbascum macrurum**, also likes sunny situations, but with a preference for open or disturbed soil.

The most famous and dramatic sections of the gorge are where it narrows and the path is confined between towering cliffs on both sides. It is here that there are many examples of chasmophytes.

Verbascum arcturus, a Cretan endemic, is a typical chasmophyte. It lacks any obvious means of deterring larger herbivores, but its flexuous, long, bright flower-spike points upwards and outwards to attract insects for pollination. However, after pollination has occurred, the fruit spike then bends downwards towards the rock face where its light, easily wind-borne seeds need to lodge.

Verbascum arcturus, flowers and fruit

Ophrys heldreichii (approx. one and a half life-size)

Verbascum macrurum
The candelabra-like structure to the left is a dead flower spike
of a previous season

One of 'the narrows' sections of the Samaria Gorge

Petromarula pinnata (Cretan endemic)

Ptilostemon chamaepeuce

Scutellaria sieberi (Cretan endemic)

Ophrys spruneri (approx. twice life-size)

In more open areas of the gorge where stable soil has accumulated, other orchids may be found such as **Ophrys holoserica** and, at lower altitudes, the rarer **Ophrys spruneri**.

Ophrys holoserica (approx. life-size)

The 'Iron Gate' narrows

After the 'Iron Gate' narrows, the gorge gradually and variably widens as one approaches the sea. The sun is by this time probably at its hottest and in places the glare from the riverbed pebbles is unpleasant. The ticket office of the National Park is reached considerably before the end of the gorge, so if one has a boat to catch it is wise not to become too comfortable with a refreshing drink at the several stalls just outside the Park. New Agia Roumeli has partly been built by those who missed their boats.

**Single flower of Delphinium staphisagria
(approx. one and a half life-size)**

150

**Looking back up the Samaria Gorge towards the National Park
(much further up the gorge than the church)**

In this section of the gorge there are many spikes of **Delphinium staphisagria**, but those used to the horticultural delphiniums will be disappointed with the rather drab range of flower colours to be found here.

A vantage point from which to grasp the sheer scale of this area is the Turkish castle, set to the north west, above New Agia Roumeli. The castle can be reached from its southern side, where there is a zigzag path that unfortunately becomes indistinct as it joins the track to the Gorge. It's almost worth getting stranded in Agia Roumeli (even if the sirocco *doesn't* blow and the boats *are* sailing) just to make the ascent to the castle in a leisurely way the next morning, whilst waiting for the ferry.

Another magnificent prospect unfolds when one is leaving by sea and the proportions of buildings to mountains are seen together.

View of the Turkish castle above Agia Roumeli

**Agia Roumeli at the entrance to the Samaria Gorge,
seen from the boat going west to Paleohora**

The boat journey back to Paleohora is a welcome rest, though any temptation to snooze should be resisted since the coastal scenery is dramatic, and its colours and shadows are enhanced by an evening sun.

The coast by Tripiti, as seen from the ferry between Agia Roumeli and Paleohora

153

12. Paleohora to Souyia and Lissos

This walk starts by taking the ferry to Souyia: in simple terms we just walk home.

The ferry takes us eastwards, past the Gialiskari beaches and Anidri hill church, which is quite a prominent feature in a sparsely inhabited landscape. When the ferry is close to the cliffs of the headland, notice the mark on the rocks, a metre or more above sea level. This is the line made when these rocks were at sea level, and is quite a startling reminder of the recent geological uplift of this area of Crete.

Leaving the boat at Souyia jetty, one turns immediately left. This is away from the village, but since our walk, with stops for flowers, antiquities and swims, can take most of the daylight hours, it is probably best to leave Souyia itself for another day. The harbour is quickly passed, with perhaps the thought that its small size, and charm, have a familiarity, reminiscent of – yes, Cornwall. But on turning right at the small pebbly beach, there is usually in Spring a display of **Malcolmia sp**. between the rocks; not an English sight!

The gorge we walk into is delightful on many counts. Its peace is often disturbed by people, but more frequently by goat bells, and sometimes by golden orioles' calls: do remember to stand still occasionally so that disturbance is not one's own.

And don't be in too much of a rush and miss the delights of **Solenopsis minuta** which flowers in the lower section of the gorge on the path sides. **Nerium oleander**, which is a common shrub of the gorge floor (where its root system is near the water table for Summer flowering) may have a few early pink flowers here.

Pinus brutia trees give some shade and a pleasant background aroma. The senses are being gently bathed, when one comes across what to me is reminiscent of a set for the film *A Passage to India*. The gorge wall rises abruptly in front of us and arches over: there is an air of unreality, and an echo.

Malcolmia sp.

Further on the path leads us out of the gorge, and once on the rim, give in to the temptation to rest. The view across the gorge is truly inspiring; a bird of prey often patrols this area, and if followed with binoculars to its perch or nest, one may then be rewarded by the beautifully delicate flowers of capers (**Capparis spinosa**) amidst their shiny bright green foliage.

Just to the right is a view to the sea through pine trees and a succession of mountainous horizons that feels contrived by a Chinese artist.

The rather eroded pathway upwards is all too obvious. It leads out on to a more plateau-like area that has little shade, but a delightful ground flora; **Calicotome villosa** and **Asphodeline lutea** being prominent contributors.

Souyia Gorge, with two walkers, and a small cairn

View towards Souyia from gorge rim

**Calicotome villosa and Asphodeline lutea
bordering the path from Souyia**

The site of Lissos

The path leads to what is virtually a cliff edge, but with a panoramic view of Lissos below.

The descent into Lissos brings one right beside the ruined 4th to 3rd century BC Hellenistic temple of Asklepios (god of healing). It is approached by several steps. The 1st century AD mosaic (after the Roman conquest of Crete in 69BC) can be viewed from the more open end opposite the altar. The siting of the temple here would have related to a spring which runs by the temple, and is now piped away from it.

Leaving the temple 'enclosure' gates, turn right, and the path leads to the 13th century church of Ayios Kyrkos, which has been partially renovated and has many frescoes. From here a path leads on past the site of a small theatre, from where one can go up to a large threshing circle (built near a change of slope where there is usually a breeze). Just to the seaward side one may see a white form of **Convolvulus althaeoides**.

Taking a path that rises slightly, and heading south west, we make our way to the barrel-vaulted tombs, of which there are many scattered on the west hillside.

Border of the mosaic in the temple of Asklepios at Lissos

Convolvulus althaeoides; white form

160

Burial chambers at Lissos

From here one can easily follow paths through fields to the beach, across the back of it, and slightly upwards to the 13th century church of Ayia Panayia, of which the main claim to fame seems to be the obvious re-use of older building materials, including a worn marble Medusa head.

Having paid due homage to the more obvious antiquities, the beach may now be enjoyed for a picnic lunch and swim. Even here one's botanical eye can be rewarded: on the cliff to the west of the beach **Campanula laciniata**'s blue bells may be seen.

Leaving such a place is rarely done with enthusiasm, especially as the only way out for the walker is *up*. An extended lunch-break can be justified by the thought that at least the sun's rays will be getting weaker as one walks back to the large threshing circle and then follows the steep path, with very little shade, westwards.

High above Lissos to the west the view becomes a more open plateau area, where one of the main ground-cover shrubs is **Lithodora hispidula** with its small blue, sometimes white, or pinkish flowers. A less frequent lax shrub is **Convolvulus oleifolius**.

Part of a Lissos field: presumably the upturned capital of a Corinthian column. Note the elaborately carved Acanthus sp. leaves

Walkers resting in shade above Lissos

Lithodora hispidula by the Lissos path

Where a track crosses the path we keep straight on over a slight watershed into quite a change of vegetation. The view behind, of the Levka Ori, gradually drops from sight; but soon, between the hills ahead, the assemblage of white dots that is Paleohora comes into view. In this area the calls of the chukar (one of the partridges) are often heard; the delight of seeing this bird here is that it's so obviously the species featured in the mosaic at Lissos.

As the path emerges at the coast, there is a very precipitous slope to the sea below. We gradually make the descent on a path that needs care due to many loose stones. When walking past an area near the sea that looks as though it has been the site of a major subsidence, do look out for **Cistus parviflorus**, which has been recorded here. By happy fortune, or by good planning on the part of the path-makers, where the path reaches the sea is a small beach known as 'Thunder Cove', an excellent place to cool off by swimming.

Cistus parviflorus

By the time the sun goes down behind the cliffs one should probably move on, since it is still approximately an hour's walk to Gialiskari Beaches. Of course as soon as one reaches the headland by the cove one is in the sun again, but the shadows are lengthening and the colours intensifying, particularly on the yellowing leaves of **Drimia maritima** (whose flowers in Autumn are borne rather dramatically on spikes, about a metre high). Gialiskari seems always to be just around the next bay's headland; but eventually one emerges, rather by surprise, from the bushes onto the beach.

The easternmost Gialiskari Beach

This is probably familiar territory (Walk 7), and whether one swims again, patronises the canteena, or marches on, one should bear in mind that Paleohora is about another hour's walk away. The path goes, as a vehicular track, from near the entrance to the Anidri Gorge: there is no path at sea level.

Asphodeline liburnica, above the western Gialiskari Beach

Bibliography

Alibertis, A. and Alibertis, C. 1989. The wild orchids of Crete. Published by the authors, Heraklion, Crete.

Baumann, H., Stearn, W.T. and Stearn, E.R. 1993. Greek Wild Flowers and plant lore in ancient Greece. The Herbert Press, London.

Blamey, M. and Grey-Wilson, C. 1993. Mediterranean Wild Flowers. HarperCollins, London.

Bonechi, C. E. 1999. The Flowers of Crete. Firenze.

Cameron, P. 1988. Fifth Edition. Blue Guide Crete. A. & C. Black, London.

Delforge, P. 1995. English Edition. Collins photo guide Orchids of Britain & Europe. HarperCollins, London.

Fisher, J. and Garvey, G. 1991 Edition. Crete the Rough Guide. Harrap Columbus, London.

Godfrey, J. and Karslake, E. 1991 Second edition. Landscapes of Western Crete. Sunflower Books, London.

Jahn, R. and Schonfelder, P. 1995. Exkursionsflora fur Kreta. Verlag Eugen Ulmer, Stuttgart.

Keyte, R. 1993. The Westwind Guide to Paleochora. Paleohora.

Pyrovolakis, N. 1998. Paleochora (A Look Back into the Past). Paleohora.

Rackham, O. and Moody, J. 1996. The making of the Cretan landscape. Manchester University Press, Manchester.

Sfikas, G. 1987. Wild flowers of Crete. Efstathiadis, Athens.

Sfikas, G. 1991. New edition. Trees and Shrubs of Greece. Efstathiadis, Athens.

Turland, N.J., Chilton, L. and Press, J.R. 1993. Flora of the Cretan area annotated checklist & atlas. The Natural History Museum, London. HMSO.

Tutin, T. G. et al. (Eds.) 1964–1980. Flora Europaea. Cambridge.

Index

Page numbers in **bold** indicate an illustration.
* indicates the species is a Cretan endemic

INDEX

173

Further Information

The following information is correct at time of going to press

The walks in this book are organised and led by me:

Jeff Collman,   Telephone: 01626 368318
21 Beechwood Avenue,
Newton Abbot,   Email: jrcollman@ukonline.co.uk
Devon.
TQ12 4LJ

I have always used specialist tour operators or their agents to arrange travel and accommodation. This not only means the ease of 'one-stop booking' but also ensures that, in the event of an unforeseen disaster, there is some infrastructure beyond the immediate hotel owner. Every year for the past 10 years I have used either one or both of the Crete specialists detailed below.

Freelance Holidays Ltd.,   Telephone: 01789 297705
Hill House,   Fax : 01789 292017
Pathlow,   Email: info@freelance-holidays.co.uk
Stratford-upon-Avon,   Website: www.freelance-holidays.co.uk
CV37 0ES

'Smart Holidays',   Telephone: 01789 267623
Holden & Leonard,   Fax : 01789 267887
Red Hill House,   Email: info@smart-holidays.co.uk
Clifford Chambers,   Website: www.smart-holidays.co.uk
Stratford-upon-Avon,
CV37 8JF

Maps of Crete are not of British Ordnance Survey standards: if they were my value as a walks leader would be diminished. The best map generally available is:

Crete 1:100,000 Touring Map Part 1 Western, Harms-ic-verlag.
ISBN 3-927468-16-9